AF130758

MIX
Papier aus verantwortungsvollen Quellen
Paper from responsible sources
FSC® C105338

Janine Franke

Teach it in English!

Implementing English in the Political Classroom

Anchor Compact

Franke, Janine: Teach it in English! Implementing English in the Political Classroom.
Hamburg, Anchor Academic Publishing 2013
Original title of the thesis: The Potential of Teaching Politics in English

Buch-ISBN: 978-3-95489-089-7
PDF-eBook-ISBN: 978-3-95489-589-2
Druck/Herstellung: Anchor Academic Publishing, Hamburg, 2013
Additionally: Technische Universität Dresden, Deutschland, Bachelorarbeit, August 2012

Bibliografische Information der Deutschen Nationalbibliothek:
Die Deutsche Nationalbibliothek verzeichnet diese Publikation in der Deutschen
Nationalbibliografie; detaillierte bibliografische Daten sind im Internet über
http://dnb.d-nb.de abrufbar

Bibliographical Information of the German National Library:
The German National Library lists this publication in the German National Bibliography.
Detailed bibliographic data can be found at: http://dnb.d-nb.de

All rights reserved. This publication may not be reproduced, stored in a retrieval system
or transmitted, in any form or by any means, electronic, mechanical, photocopying,
recording or otherwise, without the prior permission of the publishers.

Das Werk einschließlich aller seiner Teile ist urheberrechtlich geschützt. Jede Verwertung
außerhalb der Grenzen des Urheberrechtsgesetzes ist ohne Zustimmung des Verlages
unzulässig und strafbar. Dies gilt insbesondere für Vervielfältigungen, Übersetzungen,
Mikroverfilmungen und die Einspeicherung und Bearbeitung in elektronischen Systemen.

Die Wiedergabe von Gebrauchsnamen, Handelsnamen, Warenbezeichnungen usw. in
diesem Werk berechtigt auch ohne besondere Kennzeichnung nicht zu der Annahme,
dass solche Namen im Sinne der Warenzeichen- und Markenschutz-Gesetzgebung als frei
zu betrachten wären und daher von jedermann benutzt werden dürften.

Die Informationen in diesem Werk wurden mit Sorgfalt erarbeitet. Dennoch können
Fehler nicht vollständig ausgeschlossen werden und die Diplomica Verlag GmbH, die
Autoren oder Übersetzer übernehmen keine juristische Verantwortung oder irgendeine
Haftung für evtl. verbliebene fehlerhafte Angaben und deren Folgen.

Alle Rechte vorbehalten

© Anchor Academic Publishing, ein Imprint der Diplomica® Verlag GmbH
http://www.diplom.de, Hamburg 2013
Printed in Germany

Contents

1 Introduction

Within the last twenty years the concept of content and language integrated learning (CLIL) has gained enormous popularity among German schools. An increasing number of parents and students favour this approach of connecting both content and language learning as the acquisition of a foreign language in schools is often experienced as artificial and demotivating. This trend might indicate a positive development towards increased bilingual competence in different fields, such as social studies, science and technology. To support this progress, more and more teaching materials are being developed. However, many teachers are sceptic. They are afraid that by teaching their subject in another language than the students' mother tongue, they lose precious time necessary for teaching subject specific contents. The question of how an integration of language and content learning should be established is still being discussed. It is generally agreed upon the fact that CLIL is not to be considered as simple extension of foreign language learning but as interweaving of content and language – of theoretical and practical knowledge. Nevertheless emphasis is laid on subject specific contents, many teachers are not sure to what extent and in which way the foreign language as the predominant medium of instruction is to be taught. Moreover, in Saxony there neither is a curriculum, nor are there any recommendations specifically developed on the needs of different subjects taught in the integrated way. Fortunately, teachers in other federal states, especially in North-Rhine Westphalia, can already draw back on recommendations for CLIL in different subjects. As teachers from different parts of Germany exchange their experiences, ideas, concepts and materials, they establish a network that not only supports teachers but at the same time develops further different methods, models and concepts of content and language integrated learning. This relatively new concept of instruction requires teachers to be strongly committed and willing to invest extra time and work in order to turn the idea of CLIL into a successful attempt of learning and teaching. Considering the effort that has to be made, there must be a strong motivation for establishing such learning environments. Some teachers may think that by learning contents through the medium of a foreign language, foreign language acquisition happens automatically; others favour the potential of intercultural learning. In order to find out about some of the reasons why content and language integrated learning is currently being such a success in German schools, I would like to examine the example of political education in Saxony and its potential of being taught in English. For clarifying the notions applied later on, I will firstly consider the linguistic concept of bilingualism and then outline the rationale of content and language integrated learning by giving an overview of current approaches towards CLIL. Afterwards I will consider general principles and aims of political education and foreign language teaching. By analysing and comparing the Saxon curricula of the subjects English and politics I will try to find the benefits and challenges emerging from teaching politics in English.

2 The concept of bilingualism

2.1 The linguistic concept

Within academic discourse there is a great variety of attempts to define the term *bilingualism*. The definitions and descriptions try to explain the phenomenon in terms of different categories, scales and dichotomies (cf. ROMAINE, 11).

In the 1930s BLOOMFIELD considers a speaker only as bilingual if he or she gains native-like proficiency in two languages. Accordingly, the number of bilingual speakers would be strictly limited. This definition is problematic as for finding out who actually is a bilingual speaker, native-like fluencies need to be operationalised in order to measure the speaker's proficiency. However, BLOOMFIELD does not explain in what way this could be done (cf. BUTLER / HAKUTA, 114).

Another extreme approach to bilingualism is HAUGEN's understanding of the concept. In the 1950s he assumed that a bilingual speaker is an individual fluent in one language, a person who is additionally able to "produce meaningful utterances in the other language" (HAUGEN, 7.). This implies that even early second language learners can be considered as bilingual speakers. His broad view of a minimal definition is shared by many researchers of the field. HAKUTA, MACNAMARA and MOHANTY are among those who take HAUGEN's definition as basis for further addition of various degrees of proficiency in order to make the approach more precise (cf. BUTLER / HAKUTA, 114).

Another minimal definition is offered by DIEBOLD who introduces the term 'incipient bilingualism' (qtd. in ROMAINE, 11). In his description of the initial stages of contact between two languages, he refers to a passive or receptive kind of bilingualism. According to DIEBOLD, bilingualism begins with the ability to understand utterances although the speaker is still incapable of actively producing meaningful language (cf. ibid.).

By the 1990s bilingual researches shifted focus from acquisition of formal rules to communicative skills. Bilinguals were now considered as individuals or groups of people who acquire communicative skills aiming at interaction with speakers of another language. The linguistic competences of bilinguals may vary in degrees of proficiency and be applied to oral and / or written forms of language (cf. BUTLER / HAKUTA, 115). The concept of bilingualism is understood as complex psychological and social state of the individual and at the same time seen as result of interaction through two or possibly more languages (cf. ibid.). The complexity of bilingualism can easily be illustrated by the variety of dimensions applied to the concept, such as balance (similar degrees of proficiency in first and second language) and dominance (higher proficiency in one language) or early and late bilingualism (referring to the age of acquiring two or more languages) (cf. ibid., 118). These continuous dimensions can be considered for different aspects of language, as for instance reading, writing or basic interpersonal communicative skills. Besides, proficiencies may change over time. Consequently, bilingualism is of dynamic character (cf. ibid.).

It seems that these different attempts to define *bilingualism* share that the phenomenon implies knowledge, the use of more than one language and that it is a complex psychological and socio-cultural behaviour. Yet, it is arbitrary to determine when exactly a language becomes the second language. It should rather be referred to as the alternate use of two or more languages closely linked to questions of proficiency, function, alternation and interference of the languages (cf. ROMAINE, 12).

2.2 CLIL in German schools

Before I will continue with the development of content and language integrated learning in German classrooms, it is important to clarify the further use of the term *bilingual*. In the following paragraphs I will apply the terms *bilingual* and *bilingual instruction* with reference to CLIL. I will neither refer to concepts of integration of immigrants into monolingual societies as applied in the USA, nor will I refer to concepts of total immersion aiming at integration into bilingual social contexts as applied in Canada (cf. BACH, 14).

2.2.1 Development of bilingual instruction in Germany

Bilingual instruction in German classrooms roots back to the 1960s. With the establishment of the Franco-German Cooperation in 1963, the concept called "Begegnungssprache" (ibid., 9) emerged. It implied the use of foreign languages as early as in kindergartens and primary schools. The first bilingual trace with French as language of instruction was established in 1969. In the following years an increasing number of schools, especially grammar schools offered bilingual education with French but also English as language of instruction (cf. KMK, 7).

From 1980 – 1995 researchers in the field of foreign language teaching were trying to find ways of improving and optimising foreign language learning. Apart from formal aspects, activities in the classroom should now also concentrate on communicative language use within authentic contexts. One way of implementing these ideas was to declare the foreign language as medium of communication in other subjects as within this context the use of the foreign language is rather of a functional nature than of a formal one. By introducing bilingual modules, pupils were slowly familiarised with the idea of content and language integrated learning (cf. KMK, 8).

With the introduction of the European Single Market and increasing economic and cultural globalisation, English became the most important language for bilingual instruction (cf. BONNET / BREIDBACH / HALLET, 172). Linguistic and intercultural education now seems to be as important as it had never been before. As a consequence, projects of bilingual education emerge in more and more primary and secondary schools, no matter whether comprehensive, middle or grammar schools. While in 1999 there were 366 schools with bilingual education on offer, there were 847 such schools in 2006 (cf. KMK, 9). Different forms of organisation illustrate the variety of bilingual instruction offered in Germany. Apart from bilingual traces and cross-curricular CLIL modules, there are also a few schools that apply bilingualism as central tenet of their whole school organisation (cf. BOSENIUS *Bilingualer Sachfachunterricht*, 127). Since many schools are not able to offer long-term bilingual traces, they offer short-phase bilingual modules. In case of bilingual traces, students usually take part in enhanced foreign language teaching in grades five and six for preparation for the introduction of one or two bilingual subjects from grade seven to ten. In grades eleven, twelve and thirteen usually one subject is continued to be taught in the foreign language (cf. BONNET / BREIDBACH / HALLET, 172).

4

As some federal states published curricula and recommendations for bilingual education and an increasing number of universities offer special courses for future bilingual teachers the consolidation of CLIL is in progress (cf. OTTEN / WILDHAGE, 16).

2.2.2 Legitimisation of CLIL

Within the discourse of science and didactics the growing demand for CLIL is first and foremost seen as consequence of the latest international developments. Apart from processes of globalisation in science and industry, the introduction of the European Single Market led to growing social mobility between the countries. In order to be well-prepared for future challenges in their professional life, pupils need to be able to communicate in a foreign language. Foreign language competence, mobility, ability to teamwork and open-mindedness are considered the basic requirements for working and participating in the European culture (cf. Bach, 10). For this reason, there is an increasing demand for more language contact and more opportunities to use English as a means of communication (cf. NIEMEIER, 32).

Since multiliteracy is considered high value qualification within the united Europe, pupils should be enabled to study in a foreign language, develop cultural awareness and acquire strategies for getting into contact with other cultures (cf. ibid., 33). With the objectives of promoting people's proficiency in more than one language and by this providing them with new opportunities for employment, CLIL needs to be understood as an integral part of European language policy (cf. BOSENIUS *Content and Language Integrated Learning*, 15). The Common European Framework of Reference for Languages was therefore introduced as instrument for supporting the development of intercultural communicative competence by standardising language teaching methods and forms of assessment (cf. CEF). Its concept of multiliteracy includes linguistic and more general competences, such as the acquisition of knowledge, strategic competences for language learning, communicative competence and media literacy (cf. ibid, 16). Content and language integrated learning seems to offer good opportunities for achieving these aims. As lessons are mainly structured by subject matters, they provide a clear context for task- and content-oriented work that includes structured access to information and communication technology (especially the World Wide Web). Additionally, subject specific methods often rely on the ability to work with different kinds of texts, and various learning and working strategies are addressed and conveyed in the medium of the foreign language (cf. ibid., 18).

5

2.2.3 Objections to CLIL

Although CLIL seemingly offers great opportunities for fostering intercultural communicative competence and preparing pupils for their future in a globalised world, many teachers are not yet convinced of the concept. One of the reasons for their rejection roots in the organisational form of German schools. A variety of subjects determines the daily routines. This results in very limited time resources for conveying numerous contents and skills given in the curricula. Different subjects seem to be competing for precious time in order to achieve as many objectives as possible (cf. BREIDBACH *Bilinguale Didaktik*, 165). In the following paragraph I would like to discuss the most commonly mentioned objections and give some suggestions of how to cope with the anticipated problems.

Many teachers are afraid that pupils with minor language competences will be excluded from classroom discussions as they will not be able to actively participate in the foreign language. In most CLIL classrooms the foreign language is the medium of instruction. However, it is not necessary to ban the pupils' mother tongue completely from the classroom. It is not only for the reason that contents and concepts need to be acquired in both, first and second language, but also the objective of intercultural learning that justifies a well-reasoned temporary use of the mother tongue (cf. HÜBNER / GRAMMES / STORK, 240). I will discuss the role of the first language in CLIL later on.

Another common reason for scepticism is the assumption that subject specific contents are being neglected in the course of using a foreign language as medium of classroom interaction. In order to ensure that contents are well-understood, language-caused misunderstandings have to be prevented. Therefore, it would be necessary to focus on language aspects which thus would result in inferior quality of content learning (cf. ibid., 241). Although language is an important factor of CLIL, it has to be focused on in a functional way. If language mistakes do not result in misunderstandings or in disrupting the discussion, they do not need to be corrected. Emphasis should be laid on contents and language support should be offered when absolutely necessary.

Apart from these worries, some teachers even expect CLIL to have effects that strongly contradict its basic objectives. As pupils' proficiency in the foreign language is not as high as in their mother tongue, teachers are afraid that contents and problems of the subject can only be considered in a much reduced manner and thus might support and strengthen stereotypes (cf. ibid., 243). Different analyses of CLIL lessons could not prove this assumption. On the contrary, the analysis of sources in a foreign language requires careful reading and the consideration of first and foreign language concepts which fosters the acquisition of subject specific knowledge and competences (cf. ibid., 244).

The last problem I would like to mention is the idea that a foreign language as medium for classroom interaction might result in a lack of technical terms in the pupils' first language. Since the introduced concepts should be discussed from different cultural perspectives, it is useful to use the German terms when discussing specifically German associations with the term. Technical terms should be introduced in the first as well as in the foreign language.

2.2.4 The rationale of CLIL

Bilingual education is Germany is mostly offered in traces, i.e. a number of subjects (most commonly history, geography and politics) are taught in a foreign language as medium of classroom interaction. With this development a third type of language teaching emerges: it is neither a grammar-oriented, nor an exclusively content-oriented approach. The aim is to integrate both approaches with focus on conveying subject specific contents and competences via the target language. This implies a functional focus on form or negotiation of form to support the learners in precise understanding and language production in the context of the subject (cf. VOLLMER *Bilingualer Sachfachunterricht als Inhalts- und Sprachlernen*, 49). The development of language proficiency is understood as long and dynamic process including the development of discourse competence and subject literacy (cf. ibid., 56). CLIL is primarily focused on content-oriented learning. Nevertheless, the language learning process does not only include the acquisition of linguistic knowledge for mere functional and appropriate application. It also includes the development of language awareness and language learning awareness, since in the production of utterances the learner is increasingly expressing complex ideas and concepts. Only if the learner recognises the relation of form and function within the language, he or she will be able to develop discourse competence and different subject specific methods of thought (cf. ibid., 57). The challenge of bilingual instruction is to get pupils acquiring subject specific knowledge in connection with language functions of the foreign language (cf. ibid., 63).

a) The integration of content and language learning

As the improvement of both, language and subject specific competences, is the goal of CLIL, it has to be discussed in what ways language and content learning should be integrated.

OTTEN and WILDHAGE offer one approach towards this question. They provide teachers with an instructional framework for CLIL based on the following theses: First of all they claim that an integration of content and language learning in bilingual classrooms implies the use of the foreign language as language of instruction. The didactical foundations of the lesson are provided by the scientific subject, not the language. Foreign language teaching methods and concepts should support subject specific learning processes (cf. OTTEN / WILDHAGE, 24). The special value of bilingual instruction enfolds itself in the opportunity of intercultural learning by applying the foreign language. Furthermore, they state, that lexico-grammatical work has to be determined by subject specific learning processes and discourse. The further development of linguistic competence is not to be considered as mere work on vocabulary but as process of discursive character (cf. ibid., 27). Therefore, the integration of language and content for optimising subject specific teaching and learning processes implies a systematic and well-guided support of the pupil's language acquisition in complex learning situations. This includes basic interpersonal communicative skills (BICS), which should be primarily focused on in traditional foreign language classes, as well as cognitive academic linguistic proficiency (CALP) that is especially focused on in CLIL (cf. ibid., 28). According to WILDHAGE and OTTEN in CLIL teachers need to apply the principle of functional multilingualism. By working with bilingual materials pupils have the opportunity to gain insights into different cultural perspectives which should be supported by contrastive and comparing methods that foster the subject specific creation of meaning and concepts. Whether pupils use the foreign language or their mother tongue for communication depends on the specific contents and methods applied and on cognitive and communicative requirements of the respective task (cf. ibid., 31). In order to integrate language and content learning, WILDHAGE and OTTEN call for better interdisciplinary coordination, especially in terms of better cooperation between foreign language teaching and the CLIL subjects. In this context they refer to the approach called 'Language(s) Across the Curriculum' aiming at a cooperation between bilingual subjects, foreign language teaching and first language instruction. Only then language competences can optimally be transferred and thereby support the authentic use of the foreign language in bilingual classrooms (cf. ibid., 33). Cross-curricular cooperation also includes interdisciplinary methods and cooperation in terms of contents and cross-curricular work (cf. ibid., 32).

Based on these assumptions, WILDHAGE and OTTEN developed a heuristic model of CLIL which includes the explicit practice of foreign language learning in complex subject specific contexts and implicit support of language learning.

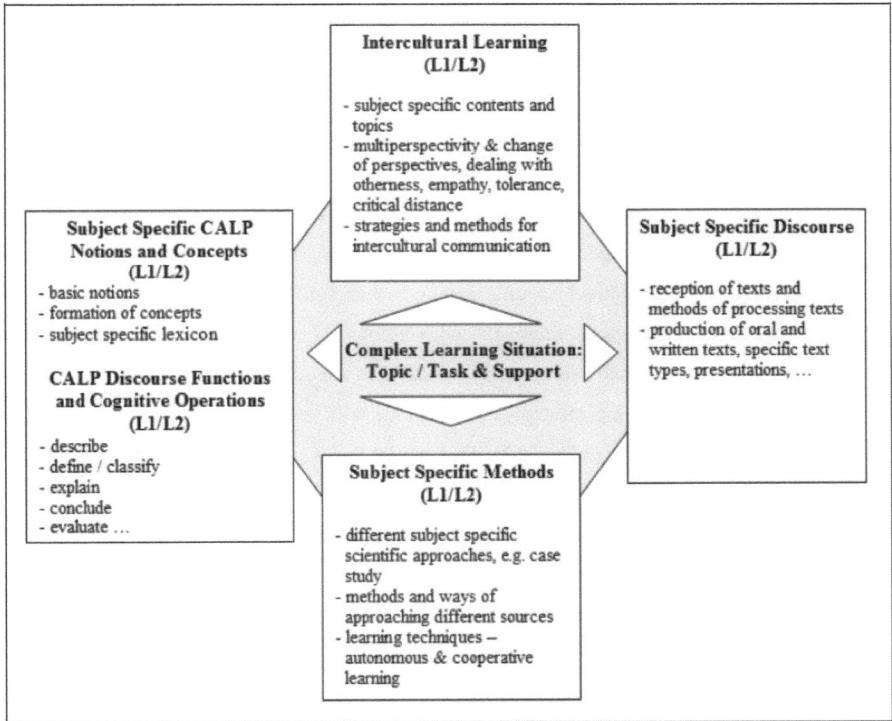

Figure 1: Integration of language and subject specific learning. Translated by Janine Franke. (cf. WILDHAGE / OTTEN, 35.)

The model also illustrates that intercultural learning should be systematically supported by CLIL. Therefore, the teacher needs to consider different cognitive and affective aspects when talking about linguistic and cultural differences in the course of CLIL in order to enable the learner to develop empathy (cf. ibid., 36). Further, CLIL supports the ability for subject specific discourse, especially in terms of receptive and productive skills and competences.

This includes different strategies of teacher and learner to recall topic related linguistic and content pre-knowledge as well as strategies of deducing meanings and strategies of processing sources of different kinds, like, for instance, skimming, scanning, receptive and detailed reading (cf. ibid.). Moreover, the model shows, that CLIL systematically supports CALP and the development of the learner's study skills by practicing and raising awareness of different study skills and at the same time providing the learner with linguistic support. Besides, CLIL fosters the development of a subject specific lexicon and encourages the pupils to exercise different cognitive operations in the foreign language while using subject specific discourse functions, such as describing and explaining (cf. ibid., 38).

Apart from this heuristic model, another important approach towards content and language integrated learning is the reflexive model developed by BREIDBACH (2007). He differentiates between 5 dimensions of bilingual didactics. The conceptual dimension refers to the acquisition of subject specific notions and concepts. The methodological dimension comprises knowledge of subject specific methods and skills. Additionally, the discursive dimension aims at developing linguistic conventions of the subject. The interactional dimension includes social and communicative skills in the classroom. At last, the reflexive dimension aims at developing strategies for dealing with experience of social and subject specific otherness (cf. VIEBROCK, 112). This model is often referred to in the discourse of intercultural learning which I will discuss later on.

The emphasis in CLIL is clearly laid on subject specific methods and contents. BOSENIUS understands subject specific learning as a combination of individual learning on the basis of the pupil's pre-knowledge and cognitive learning corresponding with the formation of subjective theories (cf. BOSENIUS *Content and Language Integrated Learning*, 18). To encourage the students to form their own hypotheses in the context of intercultural learning, they need to engage in constructive dialogues (cf. ibid., 19). BOSENIUS claims that cognitive operations of the learner are closely interrelated with the pupils' attitudes. In fact, their attitudes play an integral role in the processes of negotiating meaning (cf. ibid., 20). Therefore it is important for the learners to develop a positive affective disposition towards the group speaking the foreign language and to inspire the learner for interaction with them. In that way the pupils are enabled to psychologically an emotionally identify themselves with people of another cultural background (cf. ibid.). In the process of generating subjective hypotheses in a foreign language, the pupils face many challenges, especially as there often is a discrepancy between the learner's cognitive and linguistic abilities. Therefore, BOSENIUS argues for further language support in CLIL classrooms as WILDHAGE and OTTEN do. BOSENIUS draws on ZYDATIß' considerations about cognitive operations typical for CLIL (qtd. in BOSENIUS *Content and Language Integrated Learning*, 19):

Formation of Theory	Principles	Evaluation
Classification	Interpreting Data	Uttering opinions and preferences
Concept formation	Explaining and predicting	Weighing and evaluating
Definitions	Generating and testing hypotheses	Criticising (sources, methods)
Theorems and constructs	Generalising: cause and effect, reasons, motives means	Finding solutions and making decisions (goals, values, strategies)

Considering this table from the perspective of bilingual instruction in contrast to the perspective of traditional teaching, it seems obvious that linguistic support in CLIL classrooms is needed. As many of the cognitive strategies mentioned in the table already need to be practiced in first language instruction, it goes without saying that in bilingual lessons linguistic support has to be offered.

b) Support of language learning

Traditional foreign language teaching should enable the pupils to communicate in meaningful interactions and therefore provide the basis for further language development in the bilingual subject (cf. THÜRMANN *Eine eigenständige Methodik für den bilingualen Sachfachunterricht?*, 76). Discourse competence is essential for interaction in the classroom. Hence, language acquisition has to be supported as well. In this context, input theories (e.g. by Krashen) need to be faced critically. International student assessment programmes, such as PISA, demonstrated that performance does not only depend on input provided in classes. On the contrary, performance also depends heavily on the learner's ability to handle the specific register of language that is applied in the context of schools (cf. THÜRMANN *Zur Konstruktion von Sprachgerüsten im bilingualen Sachfachunterricht*, 139). The afore mentioned discourse functions developed by ZYDATIß' could be considered as link between subject specific contents, cognitive operations and their linguistic realisation. ZYDATIß characterises the language applied in the scientific subjects as combination of communicative and technical speech. By contrast to mere communicative register, technical language is mostly explicit, accurate, complex, structured, distant, depersonalised and independent of context and situation (cf. ibid., 140). Formal education in scientific subjects encourages pupils to speak what is usually considered as written language, no matter whether by language reception when for instance working with textbooks and diagrams or by productive tasks, such as writing summaries, lesson protocols, essays or the description of experiments (cf. ibid.). As the learner needs to practice subject specific technical speech in order to be able to participate in the discourse of the subject, emphasis needs to be laid on language output as well.

VOLMMER draws back on SWAIN's comprehensible output hypothesis. He assumes that certain learner activities lead to forming hypotheses and to reflections on the foundations of the learner's language production (cf. VOLLMER *Förderung des Spracherwerbs im bilingualen Sachfachunterricht*, 142). SWAIN states the equal importance of language input and output. Language output is of great relevance as the production of language forces the learner to switch from thinking semantically to thinking syntactically. Within the process of language production the pupils might recognise what they still do not know. Based on this insight they may concentrate on the provided input in other ways than before, paying more attention to syntactic structures and thus develop an understanding for the function of forms in the context of the specific subject (cf. in ibid., 143). The aim of a steadily improved variety of subject specific expressions and the ability for coherent argumentations, explanations and considerations can be achieved by regular practice.

VOLLMER considers learner-learner interaction, especially in small groups or pairs, as good opportunity for such practice. He claims, that by processes of negotiation of meaning the learner progresses in foreign language acquisition. With reference to the negotiating of form in CLIL classrooms, VOLLMER cannot provide an answer to questions of how and when it is best suited to correct pupils. On the one hand he argues that no correction at all reduces chances of students to draw their own relations between form and function of a language. On the other hand he mentions, that the correction of mistakes risks an interruption of the communicative situation in progress (cf. ibid., 140). By now there are not enough detailed scripts and recordings of CLIL lessons for reliable research on qualitative aspects of teacher feedback and the way learners use it. For optimised feedback in CLIL classrooms, studies on these questions are still required. However, in bilingual instruction the negotiation of meaning and mutual understanding are usually more important than language accuracy (cf. VIEBROCK, 113).

Another strategy to qualify language input suggested by VOLLMER is systematic lexical work. In order to foster the learners' discourse competence, vocabulary work should emphasise words and phrases that can be applied in subject specific discourses. They should, for instance, help to express causality, sequences, dependency, hierarchies, dynamics or comparisons. When introducing new vocabulary and phrases it is most important to apply different strategies for building semantic links between words and concepts (cf. VOLLMER *Förderung des Spracherwerbs im bilingualen Sachfachunterricht*, 133).

The formation of such cognitive networks is also important for the understanding of coherences. Complex models or concepts should be divided into their elementary parts and later on be brought together in the progress of dealing with the contents. In this way, VOLMMER argues, it can be assured that contents and concepts of gradually increased complexity are understood (cf. ibid., 135).

As in CLIL classrooms cognitive processes are triggered by interaction in the foreign language, the development of subject specific skills and methods (study skills) builds up on the learner's language skills. With regard to the problem that pupils of one class are often differing in their language skills (especially in terms of vocabulary and phrases), VOLLMER suggests to let the learners create a collection of useful vocabulary and phrases in class. If necessary, the learner can independently use this collection and thereby support him- or herself in language production (cf. ibid., 136).

THÜRMANN also claims that it is best to offer pupils options to help themselves. Discussing the aspect of systematic language support, he refers to scaffolding as appropriate tool for fostering autonomous language learning (cf. THÜRMANN *Zur Konstruktion von Sprachgerüsten im bilingualen Sachfachunterricht*, 143). Scaffolding – a metaphor for supporting the learning process – enables pupils to consciously deal with semantic fields, function and structure of text types, discourse functions and relevant linguistic aspects. In other words, it links subject specific contents, linguistic devices and cognitive operations so that learners become aware of their functions (cf. ibid., 153). Figure 2 shows an example of a scaffold for the discourse function *explaining* in bilingual geography classes. It illustrates that expectations and criteria of evaluation have to be made clear. Additionally, the tasks pupils work on should be formulated clearly and give the learner an idea of their function. To enable pupils to actively participate in the process of negotiation of meaning, teachers need to provide them with the language required, ranging from lexis to phrases and subject specific literacy (cf. ibid, 144). The aim of scaffolding is to help the students in the development of a cognitive frame for textuality and discourse functions. By using scaffolds, the pupils' study skills are reinforced and they learn to overcome occasional language problems independently (cf. ibid., 153).

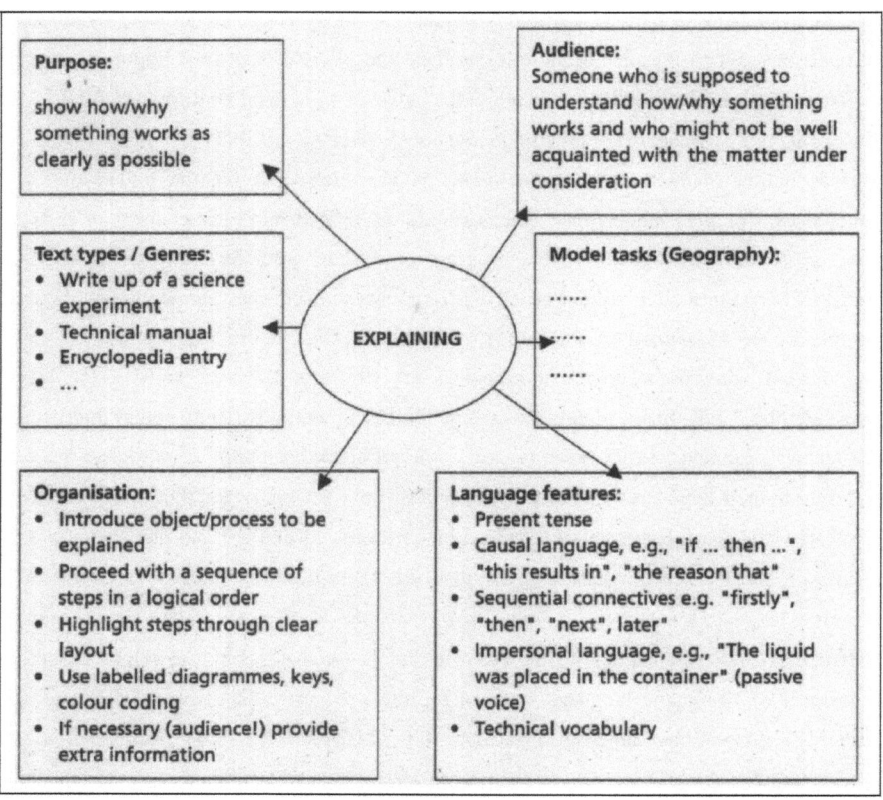

Figure 2: Scaffold for the discourse function *explaining* (ibid., 149)

c) Development of subject specific competences

Competences are generally understood as cognitive structures that determine the performance in different contexts. The acquisition of competences implies a change of these structures within the learning process. In order to specify subject specific competences, BONNET differentiates between four dimensions. According to him, the conceptual dimension is crucial for the development of subject specific competences. It comprises essential notions of subjective learning theories. This dimension is interrelated with formal aspects, as for instance rules and regularities. It is also interrelated with a pragmatic dimension referring to methods of the subject and with a reflexive dimension that comprises the path to knowledge, different methods and attitudes towards the subject (cf. BONNET, 117). He argues from a constructivist perspective that competences are acquired in interaction, i.e. when learners negotiate meaning. Within the process of interaction, pupils find out whether the meanings produced by their cognitive structures are interpreted by the interlocutor without contradiction. They are able to acquire competences when they explicate their subjective theories and modify them in case of contradiction (cf. ibid., 119). This is why BONNET suggests an integrative model of acquisition of competences which includes negotiation of meaning and interactional skills and competences (cf. ibid., 124).

The development of subject specific literacy refers to the application of different skills for specific contents within the subjects. It requires the contents to be meaningful and authentic (cf. BOSENIUS *Content-based Language Learning in der Grundschule*, 66).

d) CLIL and the importance of the mother tongue

Many teachers think that in bilingual instruction the foreign language is the only medium of interaction and that subject specific learning is inhibited as learners might easily be overstrained by the foreign language as exclusive means of communication. The explanation of complex concepts in a language pupils rarely speak outside their foreign language classes would be too difficult to understand. These ideas are often combined with the assumption that language learning should not at all be focused on in bilingual lessons as precious time needs to be used for content learning. Such attitudes prevent many teachers from engaging in CLIL projects (cf. VIEBROCK, 119). However, for successful bilingual instruction it is crucial to be aware of the fact that language is a condition sine qua non for all learning processes, since it is the medium of cognitive operation and at the same time communicative means of interactive exchange of knowledge (cf. VOLLMER 2000). In short, learning always implies language learning and cognitive learning. In foreign language learning classrooms, many teachers try to establish a learning environment that is as monolingual as possible. For the reason that many teachers claim to follow the approach of Communicative Language Teaching, the learners' first language is often considered more as a hindrance than as help (cf. BUTZKAMM / CALDWELL, 18). Maximising the use of the foreign language and minimising the use of the learners' mother tongue is on the agenda; the first language might be spoken in emergencies, especially when grammar problems need to be worked on. According to the principle of functional monolingualism, the foreign language is language of instruction, mediation and work. In other words, it is at the same time the teaching and the taught language (cf. BUTZKAMM, 91). Nevertheless, researches in foreign language acquisition have shown that the learner's mother tongue is the key and starting point for approaching other languages in all dimensions. Therefore the traditional concept of monolingualism is slowly being refuted is scientific discourse. Instead, researchers proclaim the paradox that a little less use of the foreign language in favour for occasional support in the first language might lead to better language qualifications (cf. ibid.). BUTZKAMM suggests a pendulum strategy, assuming equal importance of language and content orientation in bilingual lessons (cf. SCHLEMMINGER, 23). Therefore it would be necessary to change from focus on the subject to focus on the language and the other way round. CLIL should attempt to balance communication and language work. In this regard, language instruction is to be understood as instrument for the purpose of subject teaching. Consequently the metaphorical pendulum should be held on the side of subject-oriented communication as long as possible (cf. BUTZKAMM, 95). The mother tongue should be applied to support foreign language learning.

Periodical shifts from focus on message to focus on meaning do not necessarily imply a shift in languages. BUTZKAMM suggests different forms of well-planned co-use of the learners' first language. For early bilingual education, as for instance in kindergartens, he recommends receptive bilingualism. The child increasingly understands the foreign language but still responds in its first language. Another option for using the mother tongue in foreign language learning is the co-use of a textbook in the first language that is applied for preparation and reworking of contents at home to ensure that the learner acquires in-depth knowledge of the subject (cf. ibid., 97). It is also possible to change the language of the subject after each term. Furthermore BUTZKAMM suggests language time-outs. In this method the teacher is supposed to stick to the foreign language while selected pupils who understood everything well are allowed to explain the contents to their classmates in their first language. The fifth option he mentions is to offer an extra lesson of the bilingual subject that is taught in the first language. He does not aim at teaching the same contents in two languages. In fact fist language lessons should be used to clarify questions and problems which had not been understood in the medium of the foreign language (cf. ibid., 99). If didactically justified, it is not only acceptable to switch from foreign language to fist language communication, it can in fact be particularly advisable.

KRECHEL also emphasises the functional use of the mother tongue especially at early stages of foreign language competence. According to him, the first language should be allowed as medium of communication when complex problems can no longer be solved in the foreign language. This could apply in numerous different learning situations, for instance when consolidating subject specific concepts or when evaluating learning materials (cf. KRECHEL, 201). Unsurprisingly, there are numerous methods for conceptualising notions and contents in bilingual instruction. Some teachers consider it best to explain concepts first in the medium of the mother tongue and to work with the new contents in the foreign language later on. Others favour a parallel explanation and conceptualisation. Then there are also teachers with affection for functional monolingulism who exclusively use the medium of foreign language to explain and conceptualise contents; for clarifying language questions they provide their learners with word lists (cf. SCHLEMMINGER, 25). In order to prove the efficiency of such methods empirical studies still need to be carried out. Consequently, KRECHEL states that it is not possible to give general rules for the use of the mother tongue. Instead, the teacher has to decide which language is beneficial for the learning process within the specific context of the class (cf. KRECHEL, 201).

The use of the mother tongue can also be justified in terms of intercultural learning. When children in Germany start attending bilingual lessons, they already have internalised German notions and concepts. As such concepts vary in different cultures and languages, the learners should not only be given foreign language notions for German concepts. One objective of bilingual instruction is to let the learners form a new network of meaning; they should use foreign language notions in order to refer to concepts of the foreign culture and understand that concepts are different (cf. NIEMEIER, 37). Hence, contents referring to German culture should be discussed in German and contents referring to an English speaking country should be talked about in English. By applying their mother tongue, pupils are supposed to gain deeper insights into their own culture and extend their internalised conceptual world in their first language (cf. ibid., 38). According to NIEMEIER the process of learning about a new culture triggers pupils to start realising that their internalised arrangement of mental concepts does no longer work for the other language and culture. They gradually abandon cultural egocentrism, start acknowledging the existence of other cultures and are enabled to slowly form their second conceptual mini-world of another culture (cf. ibid. 41). Apart from acquiring subject specific knowledge and skills, intercultural learning is a central tenet of bilingual instruction. As intercultural communicative competence is one of the most important objectives of foreign language teaching in Europe, I will discuss this aspect in depth later on.

2.2.5 Teachers and learners in bilingual classrooms

Within the frame of bilingual instruction foreign language teaching is considered to be of an instrumental function. For the reason that cognitive achievements are as important as instrumental skills, learners need opportunities to develop and create communicative interactions in which they apply the foreign language. Consequently, lessons should be designed according to an action-oriented approach and offer a rich learning environment stimulating the learners' desire to communicate. Teachers and learners should see the communication in the foreign language as experiment in which hypotheses are generated and tested and in which it is allowed to make mistakes. Experimenting also implies that pupils have the opportunity to ask more questions than they give answers and that teacher and learners need to bear uncertainties and vagueness (cf. BACH, 20). The common convention of the linear process of linguistic acquisition by introduction, practice and then transfer is not always applicable in CLIL classrooms since the authenticity of language production is primarily based on subject specific contents.

Thus teachers need to be very flexible and have a language competence that goes beyond general communicative competence. In order to enable the students to acquire subject specific competences, teachers of bilingual instruction also need to be experts of the professional language their subject. Otherwise they will not be able to didactically reduce and restructure the subject specific problems, categories, concepts and their relations. It goes without saying that problems of understanding will possibly lead to anxiety and frustration in class.

Consequently, contents need to be presented in a way that learners can comprehend although the medium of communication is a foreign language (cf. BUTZKAMM, 92). Scientifically profound knowledge in foreign language and subject are as important as the teachers' cultural competence. Teachers need to be aware of the fact that each subject in each language is culture-bound. They need to be able to change cultural perspectives language- and subject-wise. Only then teachers can apply a multi-perspective methodology that enables learners to develop subject specific skills and intercultural competence (cf. BACH, 21).

Besides these requirements for individual teachers, it is also important to consider teachers in their cooperation. In order to actively involve learners in the development of authentic and demanding contents, foreign language teachers need to be informed on didactics of the bilingual subject and bilingual teachers need to be aware of specific features of foreign language learning. However, cooperation between subjects is rare. Foreign language and bilingual instruction are often only collaborating in short-term cross-curricular projects. Often the function and importance of foreign language teaching within the frame of bilingual instruction is unresolved. English classes hardly prepare pupils for bilingual lessons. At the same time foreign language classes profit from CLIL as due to increased foreign language exposure learners improve their language skills and are thus able to work on more complex tasks in English (cf. OTTEN, 218). It is therefore necessary to call for intensified cross-curricular cooperation. OTTEN suggests improving cooperation in three fields. First, he argues in favour of the Language(s) Across the Curriculum approach, stating that a collaboration between first language, foreign language and bilingual subject is necessary in order to transfer linguistic competences from one subject to another (cf. ibid., 222). Second, OTTEN favours a cross-curricular cooperation in terms of contents and topics to support intercultural learning and raise awareness of skills and strategies in intercultural communication (cf. ibid., 223). Third, he suggests that the practice of different methods should be considered as cross-curricular task since all subjects can profit from increased methodological competences of the learner.

The more methods and skills the pupils acquire, the more autonomously they can work. Especially in bilingual classrooms learner autonomy cannot be taken for granted. Time and again pupils face the problem that they do not know how to express their complex ideas in the foreign language. It is important that if such problems are encountered, they are seen as challenge to be worked on and not as unsolvable task. Yet, the emphasis in bilingual instruction is not manly laid on language learning. In consequence, the learners themselves are in great parts responsible for their language acquisition. To be able to transfer their procedural and declarative knowledge on language learning to other subjects, it is important that in regular foreign language lessons pupils gradually develop language awareness (cf. THÜRMANN *Eine eigenständige Methodik für den bilingualen Sachfachunterricht?*, 85). Content and language integrated learning can support the development of the pupils' language learning competence as well as their language and cultural awareness. To achieve these objectives, pupils need to be treated as communicators when using the foreign language in authentic communicative situations, as explorers when speaking the foreign language and as learners when using language in the observation and evaluation of learning processes (cf. ibid.).

The opportunity to increasingly work and communicate autonomously affects the motivation of the majority of learners positively. Most pupils who take part in bilingual instruction consider CLIL as motor and impetus for foreign language learning (cf. BOSENIUS *Content-based Language Learning in der Grundschule*, 66). In contrast to many teachers' fear that the foreign language as medium of interaction might scare pupils, there are a great number of learners who are in fact interested in the subject because of the foreign language; some pupils even prefer bilingual subjects to the same subject in their first language. This motivational advantage should be taken up by political education in schools. In the following discussion of political education in Saxon grammar schools I will apply the term *politics* for the subject.

3 Intercultural learning – the ideological frame of CLIL

In the age of globalisation intercultural learning is the basis for life in pluralistic societies. As migration, technological advance, the extension of the European Union and international mobility characterise life in Germany, the experience of otherness is increasingly becoming part of common everyday life. Intercultural learning is therefore of great significance in German general education. In Saxony the objectives of intercultural learning comprise knowledge about our own society, cultural traditions and developments as well as knowledge about other traditions, world views and languages (cf. COMENIUS-INSTITUT, 3). They also address the development of skills of reflection and problem-solving along with the development of tolerance and willingness to participate in a society which appreciates cultural diversity (cf. ibid., 4). EILERS describes intercultural learning as ideal sequence of phases. First, learners recognise and accept that all humans are socialised within a specific culture. Then, pupils should perceive other cultures as different without evaluating them. Finally the learners gradually develop an awareness of their own and other culture which enables them to understand their own culture from the perspective of another one (cf. EILERS, 36). Intercultural competence is the "(…) ability to interact effectively with people from cultures that we recognise as being different from our own." (BYRAM *Intercultural Competence*, 297).

In bilingual instruction intercultural competence is added with the aspect of communication. BYRAM suggests a model of intercultural communicative competence that consists of elements which can all be acquired by experience and reflection. Consequently, action-orientation and reflection need to be an important part of CLIL. According to BYRAM intercultural communicative competence manifests itself in the interdependent relation of skills, knowledge and attitudes (cf. BYRAM *Teaching and Assessing Intercultural Communicative Competence*, 33). The knowledge required for successful intercultural communication includes knowledge about other social groups, their culture and similar knowledge on one's own culture. Moreover, it is necessary to have knowledge of concepts and processes of interaction which implicitly determine the way people perceive each other (cf. ibid., 35). The skills people require for intercultural communication include the ability to discover new cultures independently and to interpret texts (in the widest sense) for somebody of another cultural background. This implies that people need to be able to identify and establish different relations between own and foreign cultural information (cf. ibid., 37). The attitudes towards people who are thought to be different are often determined by stereotypes, which does not necessarily impede the interaction. Curiosity, the awareness of own values and willingness to analyse one's own positions from other views are necessary for successful intercultural communication (cf. ibid., 34).

If stereotypes are too strong though, the interaction might fail. In the context of intercultural learning pupils need to develop a critical understanding of stereotypes and their influence on intercultural interactions. It is impossible to erase stereotypes from thinking. Social psychology has proven that stereotypes are an important filter in general human perception (cf. VOLKMANN, 88). These filters simplify, structure, organise and portion our social environment. This also applies for the perception of other cultures. As these filters cannot simply be "switched off", it is important to raise an awareness towards the way humans apply stereotypical thinking. In the classroom this can easily be illustrated by a short statement on the blackboard:

Discussion of
of the German political system

Most pupils will read *Discussion of the German political system*. The second *of* is not read as it does not fit our regular patterns of perception (cf. ibid, 89). In this way pupils can understand that stereotypes determine and guide our perception. It is important that learners are discussing their stereotypical ideas about other cultures. The new knowledge they gain can then be used to rethink these ideas and to critically reflect on them.

Intercultural learning means to constructively deal with cultural diversity. It implies empathy, tolerance and requires the learners to face others with respect and interest. In order to implement intercultural learning in bilingual instruction, the ministry of education and cultural affairs of North Rhine-Westphalia suggests contrastive learning. In contrastive learning pupils are invited to compare their own views with those of other cultures. This approach offers opportunities to change cultural perspectives, to reflect upon own views and to critically deal with prejudices and stereotypes. Hence, it fosters intercultural learning (cf. Kultusministerium des Landes Nordrhein-Westfalen, 8).

As mentioned earlier before, in CLIL it is necessary that the involved subjects cooperate. In order to find out about the potential of teaching politics through the medium of English, I will now consider the subject's objectives and analyse its current didactic conventions in relation to relevant objectives of English language teaching.

4 Politics in English: CLIL in political education in Saxon grammar schools

4.1 Objectives of political education

Wthin the frame of grammar school education, the subject politics is of special significance for general learning objectives relating to the preservation and development of our democratic society. The subject considers itself as a starting point for the learner's development to a responsible citizen who actively participates in social and political life (cf. SMK *Lehrplan Gymnasium – Gemeinschafts kunde/Rechtserziehung/Wirtschaft*, 2). Politics is therefore important for the realisation of the general educational aim of social and political participation. It strongly contributes to the objective of value orientation by supporting the learner in the development of own ideas, values and norms on the basis of our free democratic order (cf. ibid., VIII). In order to enable pupils to make responsible decisions within the frame of social pluralism, they experience the complexity of society in social, political, legal and economic contexts and gradually develop an understanding for interdependent processes involved. As part of responsible decision making the ability for reflection on perspectives and alternatives requires intelligent knowledge about social, economic, legal and political contents (cf. ibid., 2). These objectives all rely on subject specific methodological skills the pupils should acquire in the course of their politics lessons. They support the development of the pupils' linguistic competence as well as their ability to reflexively deal with different sources of information. In this respect conflict and compromise need to be understood and reflected as central phenomena of political processes which are closely interrelated with aspects of communication and tolerance. On this basis learners develop further their social and discourse competence. With reference to social competences, the subject aims at enabling the learner for empathy, intercultural competence and perspective changes. This helps to maintain and develop the pupils' identities and at the same time enables them to understand and accept other opinions and positions – a premise for life in a pluralistic society (cf. ibid). Tolerance, rational thought and own values form the basis for the development of social, political and economic judgement (cf. ibid., 3). The overall goal of political education is to support of the ability and willingness to actively contribute to our democracy. In other words, politics aims at making learners conscious of the fact that as citizens they can preserve and further develop our free democratic order – the aim is to raise political awareness.

4.1.1 Political awareness and intercultural competence

In the following I try to explain how the objective of political awareness relates to intercultural learning as frame of bilingual instruction.

Within the context of secondary school education political awareness is to be understood as mental conception of political reality. It provides political orientation and produces meaning that enables individuals to take political action and find their own judgement (cf. LANGE, 128). As integral part of the individual's civic awareness it includes ideas and concepts about how individuals are integrated in society, about generally accepted rules and principles determining life in society, about processes of social change and about the way partial interests become universally legally binding (cf. ibid.). These ideas reflect the interpretative system of society and create ideas of how to legitimise power. The meanings applied in such ideas are at the same time producers and products of basic assertions of a group of people on the political world; in other words, political culture is both frame and result of political thought, action and discourse (cf. ibid.). To raise political awareness, these aspects should be discussed in politics lessons. When pupils consciously consider the interrelation of objective structures like institutions of the political system, subjective actions and different interpretations of interests, they will increasingly comprehend political culture as active phenomenon influencing its actors and as passive phenomenon determined by various socio-cultural conditions (cf. ibid., 129). These insights can contribute to intercultural learning in two dimensions. On the one hand this knowledge can be transferred to other counties' societies and political systems. On the other hand these insights can also be discussed in reference to the concept of culture and thereby contribute to the development of cultural and intercultural awareness.

Currently the didactic discourse of political education follows a normative approach. On the basis of responsibility, rationality, objectivity and critical judgement, political awareness means to be open-minded and willing to actively take part in the democratic society. It seems to be an ideal concept of democratic awareness which automatically leads to all objectives of political education (cf. ibid., 130). However, pupils do not always develop such positive attitudes. In fact they might in some cases develop a political awareness that within our free democratic order is considered to be negative, such as affection to dogmatism or racism. For this reason political awareness needs to be understood as concept of socio-political ideas of all kinds (cf. ibid). Normative aspects of political education try to support a positive self-understanding of our parliamentary democracy. These aspects need to be reflected upon in class as on this basis learners can consciously consider advantages and disadvantages of our political system and form their own reflected values and opinions.

4.1.2 Political judgement in CLIL

Apart from political awareness political judgement is the most important prerequisite for enabling the pupils to take political action. The ability to judge is essential for the personal development of the learner. By judgements individuals define their relation to their social environment. Political judgement in particular helps learners to define their relation to politics (cf. SANDER, 75). WEINBRENNER provides a model of political judgement that can also be applied in bilingual classrooms. According to his model, political judgement is determined by six different factors. Contextual knowledge is one of these factors. As basis for rational thought it is necessary for the development of political judgement. Attitudes and values, especially conflictive values are also constituent factors (cf. WEINBRENNER, 77). Moreover, political judgement is determined by theoretical interpretations and categories which integrate knowledge and values. When dealing with their environment, people draw on subjective theories that are built on different categories. Such theories enable the individual to conceptualise different situations for easier decision making in the future (cf. ibid., 79). Political judgement is further influenced by different qualifications of the learner. Among these qualifications empathy is the starting point for basic political qualifications, such as political responsibility and social awareness. Another important qualification is tolerance and the ability to distance oneself from generally accepted norms and values, i.e. a critical social awareness (cf. ibid., 80). Impact assessment is another constituent factor of political judgement. Politics is predominantly characterised by the process of decision making with the aim of solving different problems. Hence, anticipation and assessment of possible impacts of political decisions are necessary to judge in a socially responsible and future-oriented way (cf. ibid., 81). Subjective experience is the last factor that, according to WEINBRENNER, is of crucial importance for political judgement. He claims that one specific judgement is always preceded by a number of others. The more judgement draws on generalised ideas and norms, the more differentiated and qualified it is (cf. ibid.).

This model illustrates that political judgement is a very complex individual and social process of many different variables. To get to a judgement, pupils usually connect these variables unconsciously. If contrastive and comparing methodology is applied in CLIL classrooms, learners will not only be confronted with specific situations in familiar contexts. In fact, they will also encounter these situations in different cultural contexts. For achieving better understanding of political decisions made in other countries, pupils need to be made aware of the afore mentioned factors of political judgement. In reflexive discussions learners can consciously describe the reasons for their decisions within specific situations. By working on appropriate materials or by contact with native speakers pupils can find out about reasons for certain decisions in other countries. The conscious consideration of political judgement therefore offers an opportunity for intercultural learning. In addition, it also helps to foster communicative and discourse competence since the discussion of different factors and reasons behind the pupil's judgement offers a good opportunity for meaningful interaction. A specific method that could be applied in this context is the so-called dilemma method. The student is presented with a short story containing a moral dilemma of somebody. The moral dilemma is characterised by the conflict of two equally important values. Pupils are now supposed to analyse the situations and discuss the dilemma argumentatively. They need to take the perspective of the character of the dilemma and reflect upon the person's arguments and decisions along with possible anticipated consequences (cf. REINHARDT *Handlungsorientierung*, 152). In order to support intercultural learning, pupils could consider such dilemmas contrastively: first they consider them for a German person and then for somebody of a different cultural background. Admittedly, an in-depth analysis of the intentions of somebody with other cultural roots than one's own is in most cases hardly possible as pupils usually do not have extensive knowledge about the foreign culture in focus. Nevertheless, pupils try to change perspectives and develop an understanding of other positions. For this purpose they might apply different stereotypes. These stereotypes can be taken up in the progress of further lessons and by reflexive consideration contribute to intercultural learning.

4.2 Didactic conventions of political education in relation to foreign language learning and intercultural learning

It is surprising that after more than thirty years of CLIL in German schools there are hardly any didactic considerations on bilingual instruction in politics. Although social sciences are generally accepted as well suited for bilingual instruction, history is the most prominent subject dominating the research of the field. Nevertheless, a closer look at didactic principles of political education reveals its potential for intercultural and language learning. The didactic principles named in the Saxon curriculum are problem-orientation, categorical learning, controversy as well as learner-, action-, future- and science-orientation (cf. SMK *Lehrplan Gymnasium – Gemeinschaftskunde/Rechtserziehung/Wirtschaft*, 3). If politics is taught through the medium of a foreign language, all of these principles can be related to foreign language and intercultural learning.

Problem-orientation refers to the development of problem-solving strategies and to political problems as content of lessons. Process- and problem-orientation are significant for English language teaching as well (cf. SMK *Lehrplan Gymnasium – Englisch*, 4). In the process of problem-solving learners need to acquire knowledge about the respective country and apply their new insights creatively in order to find possible solutions (cf. BREIT, 110). The particular objective of political education in this regard is to understand politics within the frame of the policy cycle: a process of problem-solving in which seemingly solved problems are the source for new upcoming challenges. Pupils should learn to identify and analyse political problems in order to evaluate them and take specific positions. Moreover, learners are expected to examine problems from different perspectives. In a micro-level approach they should take the perspectives of involved actors, in a macro-level approach they should consider the problems' implications and consequences for the whole political system (cf. ibid., 115). By engaging in these demanding tasks, pupils develop an understanding of the complexity of political problems. As in CLIL classrooms the prior medium of communication is a foreign language, such tasks are particularly challenging. Nevertheless, they can simultaneously support objectives of English language teaching and political education. Some key problems suggested by BREIT, such as the environmental crisis, inequality or chances and dangers of technological advance, are also useful for bilingual instruction since they can be applied for Germany as well as for English speaking countries (cf. ibid., 116). In the course of contrastive learning pupils gain insights into the political culture of another country and thereby improve their intercultural competence. Since different models of politics are applied for more than one country, pupils are required to repeatedly think through subject specific concepts. In consequence, subject specific learning can be fostered as well.

Another opportunity for intercultural learning is provided by the didactic principle of categorical learning. In the discourse of political education it is generally agreed upon the fact that pupils need categories for an independent analysis, structuring and reflection of political problems. On the basis of categories - like for instance, power, rule, ideology, interest, benefit or competition - pupils acquire political knowledge (cf. SMK *Lehrplan Gymnasium – Gemeinschaftskunde/Rechtserziehung/Wirtschaft*, 3). In other words, these categories are to be considered as fundamental elements forming the learner's cognitive structures (cf. HILLIGEN, 35). Within the frame of bilingual instruction, pupils need to become aware of the fact that such categories are culturally determined. Therefore politics teachers should not simply introduce these categories by mere translation of notions. Pupils should encounter such categories in meaningful contexts, i.e. when dealing with societies or political systems of different countries. In this way they can explore different understandings of the same notion and develop an awareness of cultural differences. The cognitive structures or "mental maps" developed on the basis of categories include cognitive operations, correlations and evaluative aspects (cf. REINHARDT, 28). For fostering intercultural and political learning, the cognitive models of some learners should be explicitly discussed. In this way pupils cannot only enhance their learning awareness, they can also develop further their intercultural awareness. By contrasting the "mental maps" of two or more learners of different opinions and a following reflexive discussion, pupils can be made aware of the fact that people structure the world around them according to subjective theories. Learners develop an understanding of why people perceive the world differently.

The third didactic convention, the principle of controversy, is based on the Beutelsbach Consensus. It is an agreement which proclaims the minimum standards of political education in Germany and includes three requirements for teaching politics. First, it prohibits teachers to overwhelm or manipulate pupils by imparting specific opinions. It is also prohibited to hinder learners from developing their autonomous judgement as indoctrination is unacceptable in a democratic society. Second, it declares that controversial matters of science and politics must be taught as controversial in German classrooms. Third, political education has to integrate pupils' interests. They have to be enabled to analyse political situations and ways in which other people and their own interests are affected. Additionally, pupils need to be enabled to find means to influence the political situation according to their interests in a socially responsible way (cf. GRAMMES *Kommunikative Fachdidaktik*, 242). This principle refers to a normative theory of pluralism in democratic societies. It considers democracy as attempt to organise collective learning processes which naturally include errors and mistakes. Conflicts are understood as necessary motor of social change. Therefore, errors, public discourse, opposition and controversial interests are considered as potential for new insights (cf. GRAMMES *Kontroversität*, 128). To promote pluralism there is one basic value consensus: people accept that varieties are equal in being different; in other words, members of our democratic society agree to disagree (cf. ibid., 129). Therefore, the principle of controversy especially contributes to the development of the learner's communicative competence. Since controversial topics need to be discussed controversially in the classroom, pupils develop further their discourse competence. Argumentative modes of communication are applied very often in politics lessons. Hence, bilingual instruction offers numerous opportunities to practice speaking the foreign language in meaningful interactions. Learners are furthermore likely to think about different arguments in two languages, so they consider the contents more thoroughly and thus are more likely to acquire sustainable subject specific knowledge. In short, content and language learning are integrated.

The three didactical principles I have discussed by now are all based on learner-, action-, future- and science-orientation. In regard to these didactic principles political education has a lot in common with foreign language teaching. In order to develop communicative competence in English, pupils need to learn how to use this language as tool. For this reason, they need to express themselves in authentic situations (cf. SMK *Lehrplan Gymnasium – Englisch*, 4). Action-orientation is also of crucial importance for political education. REINHARDT differentiates between three types of activities: real activities, simulated activities and productive work. The first type refers to school activities pupils engage in outside the classroom. The second type refers to different activities in the classroom. In politics action-orientation of this sort can be applied in various methods, such as role plays and simulation games. The last type emphasises active tasks in which learners are not only expected to understand but also to apply their knowledge (cf. REINHARDT *Handlungsorientierung*, 146). As in CLIL the foreign language is mostly applied as medium of communication, bilingual instruction in politics provides countless opportunities of using the language with focus on function rather than on form and thus promotes communicative competence.

In the context of foreign language teaching learner-orientation primarily aims at motivating pupils to actively use the new medium of interaction. In the frame of political education learner-orientation is also of great importance. In order to enable pupils to actively participate in our society, political education intervenes in the development of their political attitudes. Teachers need to take pupils' concepts of social and political reality as starting point for further political learning. In the progress of political education pupils then revise, differentiate and extend their ideas on the basis of new insights. They realise that their views are relevant and can therefore possibly develop a positive attitude towards political participation (cf. ACKERMANN, 77). Learner-orientation also implies that the pupil's living conditions are relevant for the subject. Classroom interaction needs to be based on personal experiences of the pupils. Through self-reflexive activities they explore and evaluate their own needs, skills, fears, strengths and weaknesses. Furthermore, pupils gain insights to what extent their experience influences processes of learning and their personal development. Gaining such self-knowledge is crucial for political education as it fosters learning awareness and provides the basis for own political opinions (cf. SCHELLE, 85). Additionally it contributes to intercultural learning. By the contrastive teaching methodology applied in bilingual politics lessons, pupils acquire knowledge about politics in Germany compared to politics in other countries. In the process of self-reflection they gradually gain insights in what ways their personal experience influences the development of their personality. If pupils comparatively consider life in other countries when working on self-reflexive tasks, they can develop an understanding that with a different cultural background, people will have other experiences and therefore their personality will be culturally different. Obviously these processes of intercultural learning are very complex. For this reason it is necessary that teachers support intercultural learning with appropriate materials and reflexive tasks which explicitly address these issues.

The last two didactic principles I would like to discuss are future- and science-orientation. In order to reach the objective of educating responsible citizens, politics needs to enable learners to autonomously consider their political and social environment (cf. SANDER *Theorie der politischen Bildung*, 17). Additionally, pupils need to be enabled to critically examine whether scientific knowledge supports or interferes with their own interests. By providing scientific knowledge of political institutions and processes that are relevant for the pupil's (future) life, science orientation should be applied for the purpose of building bridges between seemingly abstract knowledge and the learner's practical knowledge (cf. GAGEL, 157).

Pupils live in a world of institutions and systems without being aware of it. To develop an understanding of the fact that in our society lives of individuals are interrelated in a complex and abstract way, pupils need to recognise those systems and institutions which frame their own life. Only if learners develop political awareness, they will be enabled to take political action within these systems (cf. ibid., 158). The ability to take action is also an objective of foreign language teaching. Within the ideological frame of intercultural learning, pupils need to develop intercultural awareness as sine qua non necessity for intercultural communicative competence. Otherwise they will not be able to act appropriately in different situations. Apart from this parallel, the understanding of science-orientation in political education can also contribute to the development of the pupils' communicative competence. They should gain the insight that scientific knowledge is not at all fixed but instead bound to discussion and shifts of paradigm; in other words, science is controversial (cf. ibid., 166). Hence, the pupils' communicative competence can be fostered in two ways. With regard to the principle of controversy, they should discuss different scientific approaches towards the specific topic and thereby communicate through the medium of the foreign language. At the same time they can foster their communicative and learning awareness, as they should understand that knowledge can be acquired in the process of discussion. This insight also supports pupils' tolerance towards other opinions and positions as they are realised as crucial for new knowledge in the process of discourse.

4.3 Politics and language awareness

Political education can furthermore contribute to the development of the learners' language awareness. To foster political awareness, political communication needs to be discussed in the classroom. Pupils need to understand politics as human activity that aims at the creation of generally binding rules for life in society – a communicative process that institutionally frames life in our county (cf. GRAMMES *Kommunikative Fachdidaktik*, 261). Political life is determined by struggles of agenda setting and conflicts of different priorities. Our democratic argumentative culture is constituted by the continuous alternation between communication and decision. In political discourse language is used as tool for accessing and modelling reality. Notions and concepts are always associated with certain positions and historical experience (cf. ibid., 260). Political actors purposefully apply specific notions in political discourse in order to influence reality according to their interests. Hence, political communication is determined by these notions. As by communication contents of political discourse are made accessible for society, concepts which dominate the political discourse also influence the formation of political will (cf. ibid.).

Since the overall aim of political education is to prepare learners for responsible citizenship, pupils need to understand in what ways language influences their perception of reality and thus develop further their language awareness.

5 Conclusion: The potential of teaching politics in English

It has been shown, that political education is primarily characterized by controversy and discussion. Debates and the exchange of different opinions are essential for achieving the aims of political education. Hence, bilingual instruction in politics requires an advanced foreign language competence. As in Saxon grammar schools the subject politics is introduced in grade 9, teachers can draw on six years of language learning experience of the pupils. Therefore, basic communicative skills for meaningful interaction can be expected. As soon as pupils can not handle subject specific discourse methods in the foreign language, they need to be supported by the teacher in various ways, like for instance by scaffolding.

As both subjects, English and politics, are action-oriented, it is possible that English lessons support bilingual politics lessons by practicing the required discourse competences. Tasks which expect learners to autonomously analyse different conflicts, should be applied in English lessons as well. In this way pupils can be supported in the process of developing their own judgement.

In contrast to history, politics deals with current problems and conflicts in society which directly affect the learners. As topics are relevant for the pupils' personal life, they are motivated to engage in meaningful interaction and use the foreign language as medium of communication. Additionally they lose their anxiety to speak a language other than their mother tongue. The shift from learning English to learning through the medium of English helps learners to realise English as tool and not as mere subject of teaching. Because in CLIL classrooms focus is laid on message and function of language rather than on form, pupils are more likely to take the risk of making linguistic mistakes. They perceive the bilingual classroom as place of authentic communication.

Moreover, teachers in politics can use different sources which promote authenticity. Current newspaper articles or recently recorded news reports offer opportunities for contrastive learning. By using such authentic sources, pupils are presented with materials that have not especially been prepared for school education. In fact they work on media which are currently used by members of other societies. In this way political education contributes to the development of intercultural communicative competence.

The contrastive approach of bilingual instruction is also of advantage for content learning. If, for instance, pupils compare different European electoral systems, they will consider the German electoral system from new perspectives and modify their knowledge. Accordingly pupils learn to see themselves from new perspectives when reflecting upon cultural aspects and the way they determine their lives.

Furthermore, CLIL in politics promotes the development of technical terms and subject specific professional language of the pupils. The verbalisation of thought in two languages fosters cognitive structures and cognitive processes of analysing and evaluating. Dealing with authentic foreign language materials improves skills of approaching texts. With regard to language production, CLIL enables the pupils to express their complex ideas in the field of politics in English and their mother tongue.

It becomes clear that bilingual political education offers a great potential for fostering foreign language competence. As illustrated above, it also offers many opportunities for intercultural learning. In the processes of dealing with English-speaking societies and cultural traditions, pupils acquire strategies for exploring other cultures. These strategies promote comparative reflections that help learners to develop their own well-founded opinions. As in our current society cultural variety and diversity is as present as it never had been before, intercultural learning should become part and parcel of school education in all subjects. As political education offers such a great spectrum of opportunities for intercultural learning, it should be further promoted as bilingual subject. Therefore, it is necessary to develop recommendations on the basis of the Saxon curriculum. A specialised additional academic education for future bilingual politics teachers can motivate a new generation for promoting the great potential of teaching politics in English.

6 Bibliography

Ackermann, Paul. *Politikdidaktik kurzgefasst. 13 Planungsfragen für den Politikunterricht.* Schwalbach/Ts.: Wochenschau Verlag, 1994.

Bach, Gerhard. "Bilingualer Unterricht: Lernen – Lehren – Forschen." *Bilingualer Unterricht. Grundlagen, Methoden, Praxis, Perspektiven.* Eds. G. Bach / S. Niemeier. Frankfurt a. M.: Internationaler Verlag der Wissenschaften, 2000. 9-22.

Bonnet, Andreas; Breidbach, Stephan; Hallet, Wolfgang. "Fremdsprachlich handeln im Sachfach: Bilinguale Lernkonzepte." *Englischunterricht. Grundlagen und Methoden einer handlungsorientierten Unterrichtspraxis.* Eds. G. Bach / J.P. Timm. Tübingen: Narr Francke Attempto Verlag GmbH, 2009. 172-198.

Bonnet, Andreas. "Kompetenz durch Bedeutungsaushandlung – Ein integratives Modell für Bildung und sachfachliches Lernen im bilingualen Unterricht." *Didaktiken im Dialog. Konzepte des Lehrens und Wege des Lernens im bilingualen Sachfachunterricht.* Eds. A. Bonnet / S. Breidbach. Frankfurt a. M: Peter Lang GmbH, 2004. 115-126.

Bosenius, Petra. "Bilingualer Sachfachunterricht: Erträge der bisherigen Arbeit und Perspektiven für die Zukunft." *Bilinguales Lernen im interkulturellen Kontext.* Eds. M. Heine / A. Riccó / D. Schoof-Wetzig. Braunschweig: Westermann Schulbuchverlag, 2003. 127-137.

---, " 'Wir haben über Wolken gesprochen.' Content-based Language Learning in der Grundschule." *Didaktiken im Dialog. Konzepte des Lehrens und Wege des Lernens im bilingualen Sachfachunterricht.* Eds. A. Bonnet / S. Breidbach. Frankfurt a. M.: Peter Lang GmbH, 2004. 65-76.

---, "Content and Language Integrated Learning: A Model for Multiliteracy?" *Bilingualer Unterricht (CLIL) im Kontext von Sprache, Kultur und Multilingualität.* Eds. S.A. Ditze / A. Halbach. Frankfurt a. M.: Peter Lang GmbH, 2009. 15-26.

Breidbach, Stephan. "Bilinguale Didaktik – bald wieder zwischen allen Stühlen? Zu den Aussichten einer integrativen Didaktik des bilingualen Sachfachunterrichts." *Bilingualer Unterricht. Grundlagen, Methoden, Praxis, Perspektiven.* Eds. G. Bach / S. Niemeier. Frankfurt a. M.: Internationaler Verlag der Wissenschaften, 2000. 165-176.

---, *Bildung, Kultur, Wissenschaft. Reflexive Didaktik für den bilingualen Sachfachunterricht.* Münster: Waxman, 2007.

Breit, Gotthard. "Problemorientierung." *Handbuch politische Bildung. Praxis und Wissenschaft.* Ed. W. Sander. Bonn: Wochenschau Verlag, 2005. 108-125.

Butler, Yuko; Hakuta, Kenji: "Bilingualism and Second Language Acquisition." *The Handbook of Bilingualism.* Vol. 15. Oxford: The Handbook of Bilingualism, 2006. 114-144.

Butzkamm, Wolfgang; Caldwell, John A.W. *The Bilingual Reform. A Paradigm Shift in Foreign Language Teaching.* Tübingen: Gunter Narr Verlag, 2009.

Butzkamm, Wolfgang. "Über die planvolle Mitbenutzung der Muttersprache im bilingualen Sachfachunterricht." *Bilingualer Unterricht. Grundlagen, Methoden, Praxis, Perspektiven.* Eds. G. Bach / S. Niemeier. Frankfurt a. M.: Internationaler Verlag der Wissenschaften, 2000. 91-108.

Byram, Michael. "Intercultural Competence." *Routledge Encyclopedia of Language Teaching and Learning.* Ed. M. Byram. London: Routledge, 2004. 297-299.

---, *Teaching and Assessing Intercultural Communicative Competence.* Clevedon: Multilingual Matters, 1997.

Comenius-Institut. "Reform der sächsischen Lehrpläne. Eckwerte Interkulturalität." 2004. 1 July 2012 <http://195.37.90.111/apps/lehrplandb//downloads/grundsatzpapiere/ Eckwerte%20Interkulturalitaet.pdf>.

Council of Europe. "Common European Framework of Reference for Languages." 2001. 10 June 2012 <http://www.coe.int/t/dg4/linguistic/Source/Framework_EN.pdf>.

Eilers, Alke. *Politikunterricht auf Englisch. Möglichkeiten und Grenzen eines Modulansatzes.* München: GRIN Verlag, 2006.

Gagel, Walter. "Wissenschaftsorientierung." *Handbuch politische Bildung. Praxis und Wissenschaft.* Ed. W. Sander. Bonn: Wochenschau Verlag, 2005. 156-168.

Grammes, Tilman. "Kontroversität." *Handbuch politische Bildung. Praxis und Wissenschaft.* Ed. W. Sander. Bonn: Wochenschau Verlag, 2005. 126-145.

---, *Kommunikative Fachdidaktik. Schriften zur politischen Didaktik.* Opladen: Leske + Budich, 1998.

Haugen, Einar. *The Norwegian language in America; a study in bilingual behavior.* Philadelphia: University of Pennsylvania Press, 1953.

Hilligen, Wolfgang. "Kategorien als analytische Schlüsselbegriffe strukturierten Lernens." *Handbuch zur politischen Bildung.* Ed. W. Mickel. Opladen: Leske + Budrich, 1988. 34-39.

Hübner, Frauke; Grammes, Tilman; Stork, Andrea. "Bilingualer Politikunterricht: Bestandsaufnahme, Perspektiven und explorative Analyse eines Unterrichtsdokuments aus der Didaktik der Zeitgeschichte." *Didaktiken im Dialog. Konzepte des Lehrens und Wege des Lernens im bilingualen Sachfachunterricht.* Eds. A. Bonnet / S. Breidbach. Frankfurt a. M.: Peter Lang GmbH, 2004. 237-249.

KMK. "Konzepte für den bilingualen Unterricht – Erfahrungsbericht und Vorschläge zur Weiterentwicklung." Kultusministerkonferenz. 2006. 07 July 2012 <http://www. kmk.org/fileadmin/veroeffentlichungen_beschluesse/2006/2006_04_10-Konzepte-bilingualer-Unterricht.pdf>.

Krechel, Hans-Ludwig. "Bilingual Modules. Flexible Formen bilingualen Lehrens und Lernens." *Praxis des bilingualen Unterrichts*. Eds. M. Wildhage / E. Otten. Berlin: Cornelson, 2003. 194-216.

Kultusministerium des Landes Nordrhein-Westfalen. *Empfehlungen für den bilingualen deutsch-englischen Unterricht. Politik.* Düsseldorf: Ritterbach mbH, 1994.

Lange, Dirk. "Legitimieren lernen. Das Politikbewusstsein als Mittler zwischen Politischer Kultur und Politikdidaktik." *Politik kulturell verstehen. Politische Kulturforschung in der Politikdidaktik.* Eds. A. Eis, T. Opelland, C. K. Tischner. Schwalbach/Ts.: Wochenschau Verlag, 2011. 127-137.

Niemeier, Susanne. "Bilingualismus und ‚bilinguale' Bildungsgänge aus kognitiv-linguistischer Sicht." *Bilingualer Unterricht. Grundlagen, Methoden, Praxis, Perspektiven.* Eds. G. Bach / S. Niemeier. Frankfurt a. M.: Internationaler Verlag der Wissenschaften, 2000. 23-46.

Otten, Edgar. "Towards a Whole School Policy. Kooperation zwischen (Fremd)Sprach(en)unterricht und den bilingualen Sachfächern." *Praxis des bilingualen Unterrichts*. Eds. M. Wildhage / E. Otten. Berlin: Cornelson, 2003. 217-244.

Otten, Edgar; Wildhage, Manfred. "Content and Language Integrated Learning" *Praxis des bilingualen Unterrichts*. Eds. M. Wildhage / E. Otten. Berlin: Cornelson, 2003. 12-45.

Rautenhaus, Heike. "Prologmena zu einer Didaktik des bilingualen Sachfachunterrichts. Beispiel: Geschichte." *Bilingualer Unterricht. Grundlagen, Methoden, Praxis, Perspektiven.* Eds. G. Bach / S. Niemeier. Frankfurt a. M.: Internationaler Verlag der Wissenschaften, 2000. 109-120.

Reinhardt, Sibylle. *Politik-Didaktik. Praxishandbuch für die Sekundarstufe I und II.* Berlin: Cornelson Scriptor, 2005.

---, "Handlungsorientierung." *Handbuch politische Bildung. Praxis und Wissenschaft.* Ed. W. Sander. Bonn: Wochenschau Verlag, 2005. 146-155.

Romaine, Suzanne. *Bilingualism.* Oxford: Basil Blackwell Ltd., 1995.

Sander, Wolfgang. "Theorie der politischen Bildung: Geschichte – didaktische Konzeptionen – aktuelle Tendenzen und Probleme." *Handbuch politische Bildung. Praxis und Wissenschaft.* Ed. W. Sander. Bonn: Wochenschau Verlag, 2005. 13-47.

---, *Politik entdecken – Freiheit leben. Didaktische Grundlagen politischer Bildung.* Schwalbach/Ts.: Wochenschau Verlag, 2007.

Schelle, Clara. "Adressatenorientierung." *Handbuch politische Bildung. Praxis und Wissenschaft.* Ed. W. Sander. Bonn: Wochenschau Verlag, 2005. 79-92.

Schlemminger, Gérald. "Bilinguales Lehren und Lernen in der Lehrerausbildung – Ein Entwurf." *Karlsruher pädagogische Beiträge. Bilinguales Lehren und Lernen, 64.* Eds. P. Müller / W. Kosack / J. Kurtz. Karlsruhe: Pädagogische Hochschule Karlsruhe, 2006. 7-34.

SMK. "Lehrplan Gymnasium – Gemeinschaftskunde / Rechtserziehung / Wirtschaft." Sächsisches Staatsministerium für Kultus. 2007. 15 June 2012 <http://195.37.90.111/ apps/lehrplandb//downloads/lehrplaene/lp_gy_gemeinschaftskunde_rechtserziehung_ wirtschaft_2007.pdf>.

SMK. "Lehrplan Gymnasium – Englisch." Sächsisches Staatsministerium für Kultus. 2007. 15 June 2012 <http://195.37.90.111/apps/lehrplandb//downloads/lehrplaene/lp_gy_ englisch _2007.pdf>

Thürmann, Eike. "Eine eigenständige Methodik für den bilingualen Sachfachunterricht?" *Bilingualer Unterricht. Grundlagen, Methoden, Praxis, Perspektiven.* Eds. G. Bach / S. Niemeier. Frankfurt a. M.: Internationaler Verlag der Wissenschaften, 2000. 71-90.

---, "Zur Konstruktion von Sprachgerüsten im bilingualen Sachfachunterricht." *Bilingualer Sachfachunterricht in der Sekundarstufe*. Ed. S. Doff. Tübingen: Narr Verlag, 2010. 137-153.

Viebrock, Britta. "Alltagstheorien, methodisches Wissen und unterrichtliches Handeln von Lehrkräften im bilingualen Sachfachunterricht." *Bilingualer Sachfachunterricht in der Sekundarstufe*. Ed. S. Doff. Tübingen: Narr Verlag, 2010. 107-123.

Volkmann, Laurenz. *Fachdidaktik Englisch: Kultur und Sprache*. Tübingen: Narr-Verlag, 2010.

Vollmer, Helmut J. "Bilingualer Sachfachunterricht als Inhalts- und Sprachlernen." *Bilingualer Unterricht. Grundlagen, Methoden, Praxis, Perspektiven*. Eds. G. Bach / S. Niemeier. Frankfurt a. M.: Internationaler Verlag der Wissenschaften, 2000. 47-70.

Vollmer, Helmut J. "Förderung des Spracherwerbs im bilingualen Sachfachunterricht." *Bilingualer Unterricht. Grundlagen, Methoden, Praxis, Perspektiven*. Eds. G. Bach / S. Niemeier. Frankfurt a. M.: Internationaler Verlag der Wissenschaften, 2000. 131-150.

Weinbrenner, Peter. "Politische Urteilsbildung als Ziel und Inhalt des Politikunterrichts." *Politische Urteilsbildung. Zentrale Aufgabe für den Politikunterricht*. Eds. P. Massing / G. Weißeno. Schwalbach/Ts.: Wochenschau Verlag, 1997. 73-94.